AF470459

FOR ELIORA
~EH

FOR DAVID
~EB

STRIPES PUBLISHING LIMITED
An imprint of the Little Tiger Group
1 Coda Studios, 189 Munster Road, London SW6 6AW

First published in Great Britain in 2020

ISBN: 978-1-78895-208-8

A CIP catalogue record for this book is available from the British Library.

Printed and bound in China.

STP/2800/0350/0420

2 4 6 8 10 9 7 5 3 1

TALES FROM THE FOREST

WRITTEN BY
Emily Hibbs

ILLUSTRATED BY
Erin Brown

LITTLE TIGER
LONDON

CONTENTS

SPRING

SUMMER

AUTUMN

WINTER

SPRING

Caterpillar and the Flying Flower

Chomp! Munch! Crunch! Caterpillar had only hatched a few days ago, but ever since she crawled out of her tiny egg she couldn't stop eating. She'd made her way along a bendy branch, nibbling each green shoot.

Just as Caterpillar was chewing on a particularly juicy leaf, she heard the soft flutter of wings and looked up. *Wow!* The colourful creature flitting towards her was the most beautiful thing she'd ever seen!

The creature landed on a foxglove nearby, her yellow-and-black wings folded behind her. Caterpillar admired their blue tips – they were bluer than the sky! – and fiery red spots. Her colours were so vivid that Caterpillar wondered if she was some kind of flying flower. Compared to this special creature, Caterpillar felt dull with her lumpy green skin and black speckles.

"Hello, little one," said the colourful creature. She flew upwards and landed gracefully on the branch.

"Oh, hello!" said Caterpillar, pleased that the beautiful creature had chosen to greet somebody as dreary as her. She crawled closer, ashamed of her slow wriggle.

"I wish I was bright and zippy like you," said Caterpillar. "Instead of boring and slow like me."

"Well," said the creature, stretching her wings. "I've got a feeling you won't be boring and slow for much longer..."

With that she launched into the air. "Eat up, little one!" she called back.

The creature darted higher and higher until she was just a speck of yellow dancing across the sky.

"What could she mean?" Caterpillar asked herself. But then her tummy rumbled and she started munching on the juicy leaf again.

Caterpillar crawled and ate, ate and crawled, until not one leaf was left on the branch. She went to find another and began making her way through the shoots there. The branch sagged under her weight – she was getting bigger! Days passed and Caterpillar stripped the shrub of almost all its leaves. Finally she didn't feel like eating any more.

"Perhaps this is what that creature meant," thought Caterpillar. "I do feel like something is about to change..."

She found a sheltered branch and spun a silk thread to hang from. Caterpillar shimmied off her outer layer of skin, revealing a brown case – a special chrysalis. On the outside it was as motionless as a dead leaf, but inside something amazing was happening...

For two weeks, the chrysalis remained quiet and still. Then, one morning, it split apart, like a bud opening its petals. A beautiful creature emerged, flashing with yellow-and-black patterns. Dashes of brilliant blue and vivid red decorated her wing tips. Caterpillar had become Butterfly!

"I'm just as bright as that creature that settled beside me," she said. "I hope I'm as zippy as her too!"

Butterfly opened up her wonderful wings and set off into the sky. She certainly wasn't slow and boring any more.

"I crawled around, ate every leaf within range,
Became a chrysalis and started to change.
Now I'm a butterfly, what a sensation –
It's nature's most amazing transformation!"

Adder's Itch

The sun slid out from behind the clouds. Slowly, Adder unwound his coils and stretched out on his favourite basking rock. Heat seeped through his skin and spread across his whole body. The wonderful warmth was such a relief after spending the bitter winter curled up in a burrow below ground! Adder's dark tongue flicked out to taste the air. He scented dead bracken, rain-soaked soil and the musky odour of a small, warm-blooded creature nearby. The creature smelled yummy but there would be time to eat later after he was properly warmed up!

As Adder lay sunbathing he became aware of an itching, tickling, prickling feeling.

"Why is my skin so tight?" he hissed. Adder tried to ignore it and enjoy the sunshine, but the itchiness got worse.

"Perhaps my skin has shrunk in the sun," he said. "I'll go for a slither and see if it stretches out again."

Adder slid off the rock into the crackly bracken. His black-and-white zigzags faded into the undergrowth as he wriggled along, trying to stretch his skin.

"Maybe I'll have a snack," Adder said. "That'll take my mind off things."

He pressed his head to the ground and felt for the vibrations of paws scurrying beneath the soil. Yes! He could sense a little shrew inside a burrow below. But then Adder felt a different sort of vibration – the smooth, slithery movements of a snake... A sleek body slid out from between the branches of bracken. It was another adder!

"That smells tasty," said the stranger. "I'll fight you for it!"

Adder hissed. He was already feeling cross about his itchy skin – he didn't need another snake attempting to steal his snack too! He reared up off the ground so half of his body stood upright. The stranger mirrored him and the two snakes twined together, looping round and round. Their intricate dance moved them across the forest floor, as each adder tried to prove that he was stronger and push the other to the ground. Adder pushed with all his might, forcing the stranger down.

"OK, OK. You win, I'll go!" said the other snake as he slithered away. Adder had won, and better still…

"My skin doesn't feel so tight now," said Adder. He twisted round and saw that the thin, scaly skin of his tail was beginning to lift away from the layer underneath. It must have rubbed off during the dance.

Of course – he needed to shed his skin!

It had been such a long time since he'd last shed – before the winter hibernation – that he'd forgotten that was what the itching, prickling, ticking feeling meant. Adder rubbed his head against a rock. He scraped and he scratched and he scuffed until the skin loosened enough for him to slither out of it completely. Lying in the bracken, the pale husk of his old skin dried out in the sun. Adder slid away, his shiny patterns gleaming brightly.

"My patterned scales are stretchy and strong,
They'll grow with me until I get too long.
Then twice a year, in the autumn and spring,
I'll rub and I'll scrub and I'll shed my skin!"

The Woodpeckers' New Home

The woodpeckers were worried. It was nearly time for She-Woodpecker to lay her eggs but their neighbourhood was full of dangers. Cunning crows nested next door and crafty foxes had dug a den right at the base of their tree.

Crows and foxes didn't frighten the woodpeckers – but they weren't the sorts of beady-eyed creatures they wanted nearby when their little ones were learning to fly. If a fledgling took a tumble to the forest floor, they might… The woodpeckers didn't want to think about it!

"We're going to have to move," said She-Woodpecker one spring morning. "This is not the right place to bring up our chicks – there are too many dangers."

He-Woodpecker agreed and they set off in search of a new tree to call home. They flew through the forest, looking from one tree to the next.

"Kek! Kek!" called She-Woodpecker, spotting an ancient oak tree with roots like rivers running across the forest floor. "Come and look at this one."

He-Woodpecker flew over and landed on a branch. He gave the trunk a few sharp pecks, but even his chisel-like beak couldn't break through the tough bark.

"No good," he said. "The wood is too hard. We'll have to keep looking."

The pair set off once more, searching high and low for the perfect place to peck a new nest.

"This one looks softer," called He-Woodpecker. He landed on the trunk of a younger oak, its wibbly leaves fresh and green. Toes spread to keep him steady, He-Woodpecker gave the bark a sharp peck. He drilled through the wood straight away.

"This is the one!" he said.

"I'm not so sure..." said She-Woodpecker. She landed on a higher branch and peered into a hollow on the side of the tree.

There was a shrill squeak. A flurry of red fur. And the whip of a big, bushy tail.

Uh-oh!

"I think this tree is already taken," She-Woodpecker said, flapping backwards as a fierce mother squirrel shooed her away from her drey. She clearly didn't want to share.

The tired woodpeckers flew on, covering many miles as the sun slid across the sky. Finally they spotted a thick, gnarled tree that seemed to stretch all the way up to the clouds. Its bark was broken and flaky and, better still, the woodpeckers couldn't see any unwelcoming neighbours. They perched on the trunk and gave it a few probing pecks. It was perfect!

Together they struck the wood with their beaks, again and again and again, working to create a little hole. They pecked so fast their beaks became a blur. Wood chips fell to the forest floor like snowflakes, making a little heap beneath the new hollow. As they pecked, the hole got bigger, and bigger, and BIGGER. But nest-building was hungry work.

"I'll see if I can find us a snack," said She-Woodpecker after a few hours.

While He-Woodpecker worked on their new home, She-Woodpecker shuffled down the trunk, tapping here and there.

Beneath the bark, the tree was teeming with wood-boring beetles. Delicious! Her long tongue licked up a few tasty creatures. She collected a few more in her beak and flew back up to share them with He-Woodpecker.

"We've chosen a top spot," she said with a mouthful of yummy bugs.

Over the next few days, the woodpeckers pecked away until their hollow was ready. The round opening was just about big enough for them to squeeze through one at a time. Inside was a deep and cosy cavity, lined with wood chippings. There was plenty of room for a new family.

"Before we settle in, I'll let everyone know that this is *our* spot," said He-Woodpecker.

He flapped out on to a dead branch, half-snapped and hanging low to the ground, and began hammering the wood with his beak. The red nape of his neck bobbed backwards and forwards as he pecked.

Tok, tok, tok, tok, tok! Tok, tok, tok, tok, tok!

The loud drumming echoed around the forest. Now all the animals knew that this was the woodpeckers' tree.

A few days later, She-Woodpecker laid six smooth, shiny eggs. They sat at the bottom of the nest cavity.

"They're beautiful," said He-Woodpecker.

She-Woodpecker nestled on top of them, so the eggs would stay snug. "It won't be long before they hatch..."

Every day the woodpeckers took it in turns looking after the eggs and searching for food, swapping roles as the sun set and rose. After a few weeks, their teamwork paid off.

One morning, a crack as thin as a spider's silk thread appeared on the surface of the biggest egg. Soon the crack grew to the width of a blade of grass and, not long after, a tiny, hungry beak appeared. By the end of the day, there were five more mini mouths to feed.

"Hello, little ones," said She-Woodpecker as the chicks chirruped.

He-Woodpecker arrived back at the nest with a beakful of worms to share with his new family.

"Welcome to the world," he said proudly. "Now, eat up. You've got a lot of growing to do!"

"We searched the forest for the perfect tree,
Then pecked a new home for our family.
Now our tiny chicks can grow, feed and rest,
Until, feathered and fledged, they fly the nest."

Rabbit Across the River

Rabbit sat on the riverbank staring at the meadow across the water. Her head was tilted to one side, and her two usually floppy ears stuck straight up.

"Is it just me," said Rabbit to herself, "or does the grass over there look much lusher than the grass here?"

The thistles were bushier and the leaves juicier too. Across the river the dandelions glowed like little suns.

Over there, everything looked bigger, brighter and yummier.

Rabbit glanced back at the entrance to her burrow, just visible at the edge of the trees. She could see the other does and bucks beginning to emerge. Every day at dawn and dusk Rabbit foraged in those woods with them, searching for the same old boring shrubs and greens.

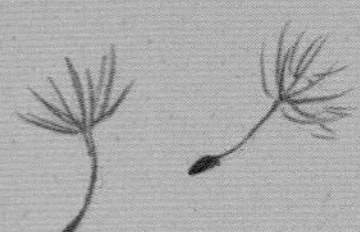

"Why should I stay on this side when the other side is so much better?" she wondered.

The sky blushed cherry-blossom pink as the sun sank lower. Rabbit made up her mind. She was going to hop over to the other side of the river and munch on the grass in the meadow. She bounced to the water's edge and on to the stepping stones.

Hop! Hop! Hop – whoops! Her paw slid on some slimy plants and she nearly tumbled into the water! Rabbit scrabbled until both paws were firmly back on the stepping stone. She made it to the next one, then the next one, until…

"I did it!" Rabbit said as she sprang on to the other bank and looked around. "And it's even better here than I thought."

The grass swayed in ribbons of emerald green. Bright flowers dotted the meadow. Straight away Rabbit began munching on a delicious-looking dandelion leaf. When she'd sampled a dozen dandelions, Rabbit moved on to the thistles. They were fresh and very crunchy. Next she began to nibble on the swaying grass.

"This is much tastier than the grass on my side of the river," she said.

Above her, the sun sank lower and lower, until it was just a golden glimmer on the horizon. Gloomy grey

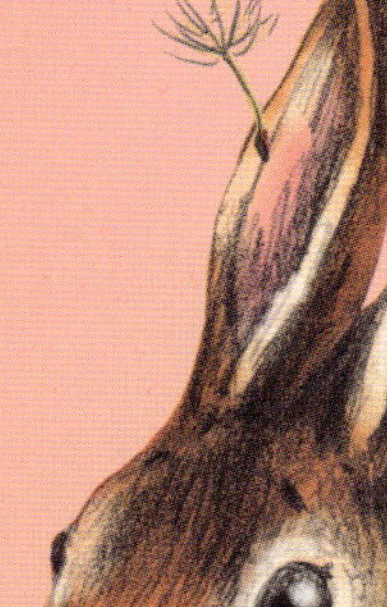

clouds swept in to take its place. Rabbit was too busy munching to notice the darkness falling around her.

A drop of rain plopped on to Rabbit's twitching nose. Drip! Drip! DROP! Soon Rabbit couldn't ignore the rain any longer.

"I'll shelter in that bramble patch," she said. "Once it's stopped drizzling, I'll head back to my burrow."

Rabbit wriggled between the spiky stems, being careful to avoid the thorns. She used her front paws to dig. It was tough going as Rabbit's claws kept striking big stones – the soil wasn't the best kind for digging in. Still, she managed to make a little hideaway where she fell asleep.

While Rabbit snoozed, the storm clouds gathered. The drizzle turned to a downpour.

When Rabbit awoke, the stars peeked out between the tiny gaps in the grey clouds. The rain was still falling heavily.

"Whoops," said Rabbit. "I only meant to kip for a minute! I should be getting back to my burrow."

She bounded to the riverbank, ready to jump across…

But where had the stepping stones gone?

They'd disappeared! All that rain had caused the river to rise. Water gushed right up to the bank, splashing Rabbit's front paws. There was no way she could get back over.

If she tried to swim, those currents would surely sweep her away. What was she going to do?

"I'll have to dig a burrow, but it will be hard work without my sisters, cousins and aunties to help me," she said. Across the river, her wonderful warren was full of chambers and tunnels, with plenty of room for the whole colony to shelter from the rain. It had taken all the does' hard work to get it just right.

Rabbit hopped back to the bramble patch and began to dig, scraping at the stony soil until her hideaway became a shallow burrow. Rabbit wriggled into the small space and tried to settle down. But it was scary being in a new place away from the safety of her warren! There were so many strange noises and smells. Was that the stinky scent of Stoat? Was that the rustling of Hawk's wings? Her burrow wasn't deep enough to offer much protection if any predators came snooping.

As the rain pitter-pattered above, a horrible thought struck Rabbit. "What if I can never get back?" she said. She thumped her foot against the ground in alarm. Perhaps the river would stay rushing and gushing like this forever. Perhaps the stepping stones would never reappear. With these thoughts whirring around her head, it took a long time for Rabbit to get to sleep. Finally she settled down.

Rabbit woke up to the sounds of chirps and chatters. Songbirds hidden in the branches of her thicket were saying good morning to each other, as they did every day at dawn. Rabbit scrambled out of the burrow to see the meadow glittering with beads of dew. The rain had stopped and only a few wispy clouds smudged the sky above her.

Almost too frightened to look, Rabbit hopped to the water's edge. The river was much lower and she could see the surface of the stepping stones. Rabbit could go home!

Hop! Hop! Hop! Her fluffy tail flicked as she leaped carefully from stone to stone. When Rabbit scrambled up on the opposite bank, it seemed more beautiful than it ever had before. The thistles looked fresh, the leaves juicy and the dandelions glowed brighter than the brilliant morning sun. She did a binky in the air, her back legs flying out behind her as she bounded towards her warren. Outside the entrance, Rabbit stopped to munch on a green blade. "I suppose the grass here is pretty tasty, after all."

"I love to munch grass wherever I roam,
But it's best to stay near my underground home!
When danger is near, I can thump my feet –
A signal to others that we should retreat!"

The Little Cub Who Could

"You want me to climb down there?" asked Little Cub, peering out of the tree hollow. The young bear could hardly see a thing. Puffs of white mist veiled the world below.

"That's right. There's a whole forest hidden down there, I promise," said Mummy Sow.

Little Cub wasn't sure. This snug tree hollow was her whole world! She'd spent the first few months of her life here, cuddled up with Mummy Sow. But now the weather was getting warmer and it was time for them to leave.

"I'll go first," Mummy Sow reassured her.

Little Cub felt her paws tremble at the thought of stepping into nothing. Mummy Sow swung out on to the tree, navigating the bumps and lumps as she made her way down the trunk. She soon disappeared beneath the mist.

"Come on, Little Cub," she called.

"I can't do it, Mummy!" Little Cub said. She was too frightened!

Mummy Sow poked her nose back up through the fog. "Yes, you can. Just place one paw at a time." The sight of her face made Little Cub feel braver. She scrambled out of the hollow and dug her sharp claws into the trunk.

"One paw at a time," Little Cub repeated as she slowly shuffled down the bark. She kept her eyes fixed on the tree.

"That's it," said Mummy Sow. Down Little Cub climbed until – bump! – her bottom hit the floor. She had done it! Mummy Sow was right – here was a big wide world. Sprouts of greenery shot up through the muddy forest floor.

"I told you that you could do it," said Mummy Sow.

Mummy Sow set off through the trees with Little Cub bounding along behind. Soon the pair reached a roaring river. Little Cub sneezed as the icy spray splashed her nose.

"We're going to swim across," said Mummy Sow.

"Across the rushy, roary, icy water?" asked Little Cub. "Surely we'll be swept away!"

"Follow me," Mummy Sow called as she waded in. But Little Cub kept her paws rooted on the bank.

Mummy Sow dipped her nose under the water, paddled with her powerful legs and soon reached the other side.

"Come on, Little Cub," called Mummy Sow.

"I can't do it, Mummy!" said Little Cub. She was too frightened!

"Just kick one leg at a time," Mummy Sow said.

With a deep breath, Little Cub plunged into the river. Although the water rushed around her, with a few powerful kicks she moved through it easily. Little Cub reached the other bank. She splashed out beside Mummy Sow.

"I told you that you could do it," said Mummy Sow.

As they walked on along the bank, the morning mist lifted and the sunshine glittered off the water. Little Cub kept noticing strange splashes and the flash of shiny, scaled bodies. Mummy Sow told her they were called fish.

"Are you hungry, Little Cub?" asked Mummy Sow.

"A bit," said Little Cub. She shuffled forwards, ready to drink some milk.

"No milk today," said Mummy Sow. "We're going to catch a fish."

"One of those quick, slick, splashy things?" asked Little Cub. They were so fast!

"Yes," said Mummy Sow. "Watch me."

Once again Mummy Sow waded into the river. She planted her paws and watched

the water until ... *fizz-hiss*! She snatched a salmon from the bubbling flow.

"Your turn, Little Cub," said Mummy Sow.

"I can't do it, Mummy!" said Little Cub. She was too frightened!

"Yes, you can. Just make one swipe at a time."

Little Cub followed Mummy Sow back into the water. She spotted the flash of a fin and lunged. She missed! But here came another one... Time and time again the fish squirmed out of Little Cub's grasp but she didn't give up. Until finally – *fizz-hiss!* – Little Cub snatched up a fish and wrapped her jaws round it. It was delicious!

"I told you that you could do it," said Mummy Sow. "I taught you these things so that when you're older and the frosts arrive you'll be able to find a cosy cave or hollow, all by yourself, and cuddle up for the winter."

"Without you?" Little Cub asked. There was no way she'd be able to do that. She was too frightened! "I can't do it, Mummy!"

"Could you climb a tree?" said Mummy Sow.

"Yes, but—"

"Could you swim across a river?"

"Yes, but—"

"Could you catch a fish?"

"Yes, but—"

"Then you can survive the long winter sleep all by yourself. I know you can."

Little Cub looked into Mummy Sow's eyes. "OK, Mummy. I can do it."

Spring slipped into summer. Mummy Sow taught Little Cub to forage for grubs and berries, run from danger and find the best plants for bedding. By the time the nights began to lengthen, Little Cub wasn't so little any more. Too big to cuddle up in the hollow, the bears found a cave to snooze in through the cold months. When spring arrived, they returned to the woods. It was time for Cub to set off alone.

Cub explored far and wide as the summer wore on. When winter came she ate as much as she could, gathered bedding and found a cave, just as she'd been taught. As the winds blew, Cub curled up and closed her eyes.

"My sharp claws have grown, I can climb any tree,
Swimming across the river doesn't scare me.
I can catch a fish in my powerful jaws,
And now I'll fill this cave with noisy snores!"

SUMMER

 Bee's Treasure Hunt 

Bee's wings hummed an excited song as she buzzed over to the tunnel that led into the forest. Since hatching a few weeks ago Bee had been helping in the hive, cleaning up the honey storage cells and looking after the new bee babies. Today, for the first time, she was heading outside.

"Hello, Bee!" said her friend, joining her. "It's your first day gathering food, isn't it?"

"Yes!" said Bee. "I don't know exactly what to do..."

"I'll help you," said her friend. "It's like a treasure hunt. We have to find the best food and bring it back to the hive."

Another forager bee landed at the hive's entrance, returning from her morning mission. The forager began to wiggle, wobble, whirr and buzz. There was a secret message hidden in her movements that told the next gathering group where they could find the fluffiest pollen and juiciest nectar! Bee pressed up against her. From the forager's dance, she

could tell which direction she should fly in and how far.

Bee and her friend buzzed out of the hive into the bright blue sky. They followed the directions in the forager's movements, winding along the river before veering off to the east. Finally they reached a glade and zipped down into the swooshy grass, scattered with purple-petalled blooms.

"This looks like a good one," said Bee's friend, settling on a flower with a yellow star at its centre. Bee landed beside her.

"I'll collect the nectar, you gather the pollen," her friend said. She began sipping on the sweet nectar in the flower's centre.

"Don't you need to take it back to the hive?" asked Bee.

"I'll keep it safe in my tummy," said her friend. "When we get back, I'll pass it on to other bees to turn it into honey. Then we'll store it until the winter so there's plenty of food when the flowers have gone."

Bee spotted some bobbly orange pollen at the top of the flower's anthers. She climbed up and the pollen clung to the tiny hairs all over her body.

"That's it!" said her friend. "Now comb it down on to your hind legs."

Bee brushed the powder on to her

legs, where it stuck in two little pockets.

"Once you've collected more you can take it back to the hive to be made into bee bread!"

The pair set off to find another flower. Soon Bee had a heavy orange orb attached to each hind leg and her friend had a tummy full of nectar. They whizzed back to the hive and passed on their pollen and nectar to the others. Bee looked around at their busy home, bursting with hundreds of workers going about their jobs. The walls gleamed with honey stores and pollen pockets, bathing the whole hive in a soft golden glow.

She couldn't wait to set out again tomorrow and bring back more treasure!

"Each bee has a role within our home,
From forager to nurse, queen to drone.
The swarm harvests honey all summer long,
Working hard to keep the hive strong!"

Night of the Fireflies

Firefly should really be getting back. He had spent the day flitting through the forest, racing beetles and butterflies, stopping to nibble on some pollen. He had flown all the way to the river, resting on its bank as water rushed and roared past. But as the sun sank low in the sky, oozing orange light across the horizon, he knew he needed to re-join the swarm. Twilight was a special time for fireflies.

Wings humming, he began to make his way through the towering trees. It seemed a long and lonely journey now there were no other insects to race.

The shadows grew as gloom settled. Firefly buzzed and bumbled, trying to remember which way to go.

"This would be a lot easier if I could just ask one of the swarm," said Firefly. But none of his friends appeared. He supposed they were still gathered in the glade he'd left this morning when he'd set out on his solo adventure.

Now he had no idea where that was, or how he might find it. He was lost!

Firefly tried to unjumble his thoughts.

"I know!" he said. "I'll hover up high, then I might be able to spot one or two fireflies flitting above the trees – the swarm won't be far below!"

So up he buzzed, until he could see the whole wood stretching out beneath him.

But what was that? In a clearing not far ahead, it looked like the stars had fallen down into the forest! A million glimmering lights hovered in the air below him. The lights flashed in a steady rhythm, as if they were all moving to a silent symphony.

Firefly set off to investigate. Closer and closer he went, peering at the flashing stars to try to work out what they could be. The winking lights whizzed around, painting the darkness with bright brushstrokes. There was a pattern to their flashes that seemed strangely familiar to Firefly…

"Join in, Firefly!" called a voice from below. It sounded like one of his friends.

It was the swarm! He'd always been within it before, so he'd never had a chance to see the special sight from the outside.

The fireflies were using their tail torches to create a light display, flickering on and off all at the same time.

He turned on his own tail torch and felt the familiar fizz as it began to glow.

"Bet you can't shine as bright as me!" called a voice from the darkness again.

"No, my light's the brightest!" said another voice.

"No, mine is!" said another.

Firefly's light flickered like a little golden star at the end of his tail. He swooped down to join the swarm. If he ever got lost again, he just needed to look for the fallen stars of the forest!

"Here I come!" he said. "And my light is the brightest of all!"

"Born underground, we rise for a reason,
To spread our wings for one sunny season.
When evening falls, we each flash a light —
The stars of the forest, burning bright."

The Very Best Boar

"How many times do I have to tell you?" said East Boar. "This muddy pool is on *my* side of the forest."

West Boar tossed back his tawny head. "No," he said. "It's on MY side of the forest."

The two boars had been arguing over the pool all summer. They lived alone on opposite sides of the wood and usually avoided each other. But this gloopy, soupy pool of mud was right between their territories. It was the perfect place to wallow on warm nights like this one and neither boar wanted to give it up.

"It's mine!" roared East Boar.

"It's mine!" rumbled West Boar.

The two boars began to circle round, sizing each other up. Normally boars resolved arguments by fighting – jabbing their sharp tusks to try to spear the other. But neither boar would make the first move…

"It's too hot for this," said East Boar eventually. "Can't we settle it another way?"

West Boar thought for a moment. "Whoever is the best boar should get the pool."

"But how can we decide who's the best boar without fighting?" asked East Boar.

West Boar thought again. What were boars brilliant at? And, more importantly, what was *he* brilliant at…

Aha! "Whoever can charge the fastest!"

That sounded fine to East Boar. He was excellent at charging.

West Boar allowed his rival to cross the border into his territory and the two boars stood shoulder to shoulder, facing a weeping willow.

"First to the tree wins the pool," said West Boar. "Three, two, one … go!"

Dirt flew in all directions as the two pigs thundered towards the willow. East Boar's tusk touched the trunk of the tree a second before West Boar's.

"The pool is mine!" East Boar declared.

"Not so fast," said West Boar. He was disappointed not to have won, but he quickly came up with another idea. "Any creature can charge, but only *boars* can bellow. Whoever has the loudest bellow should get the pool."

East Boar grunted. He'd won the charge fair and square! But his bellow was pretty impressive. He supposed it wouldn't hurt to prove it.

"I'll go first," he said. East Boar planted his feet in the dusty earth and roared with all his might. The sound sent birds scattering from the trees.

"Not bad," said West Boar. "But listen to this."

He took a gulp of air, then bellowed so loudly the water in the pool wobbled in wide ripples. For a moment the whole forest was silent, as if in shock.

"The pool is mine!" West Boar announced.

"Wait a minute!" said East Boar. "Being able to bellow isn't the best test of being a good boar. We should see who can root up the most grubs. That will really decide it."

West Boar shook his tusks. Surely his brilliant bellow proved that he deserved the pool? Then again, he was very good at rooting for grubs – and he was getting hungry!

The boars picked a spot among the trees and used their strong snouts to turn over the soil, searching for creeping, crawling things beneath the dirt.

"Got one," East Boar called.

"Me too!" West Boar replied, his mouth full.

On they went, matching grub for grub, with neither able to get ahead of the other. Eventually they were so full that they decided to stop foraging.

"Well," said East Boar. "I suppose that one is a draw."

The two boars flopped down in the dirt, exhausted. But the question still remained over who should get the pool. They'd each won one of the three challenges, and the last competition had been a tie!

"That's a noble bellow you have," admitted East Boar.

"Your charge was pretty powerful," replied West Boar.

"And we were both fantastic at foraging for grubs," said East Boar.

"What a pair of impressive boars we are!" said West Boar.

But who should get the pool? They stared at the muddy water, spotted with starlight. The wind blew and the reeds at the water's edge rustled invitingly.

"I suppose it wouldn't be the worst thing in the world –" started East Boar.

"– if we just shared the pool," finished West Boar.

East Boar grunted his agreement.

The boars heaved themselves off the ground.

Beneath the moon, they wallowed in the mud until morning. As it turned out, the gloopy, soupy pool was big enough for them both.

"Our tusks are sharp, our bellows are loud,
Old boars live alone – two is a crowd!
But on warm nights, when the moon is high,
You might spot us wallowing side by side."

BAT IN A FLAP

Summer was in full swing. The golden sun shone brightly and flowers unfurled their petals to lap up its light. Animals across the forest lolled and lazed in shady spots. Birds darted across the cornflower sky and insects hummed from one ripe fruit to the next. It seemed like everybody was out enjoying the dazzling day. Everybody, except Bat.

Bat could not get back to sleep! He had woken to find his usually gloomy roost bathed in bright sunshine. Worse still, the air was thick, sticky and far too warm. Not good conditions for snoozing at all! Outside, he could hear birds chattering and the scurrying of feet across the forest floor.

"This won't do," he said. "It's hours and hours until moon rise. I should be fast asleep!"

Edging his hooked feet further into the hollow, he turned his back on the sizzling sun. He rustled and shuffled,

wriggled and jiggled, and tried to get comfy.

"I'll be dozing in no time," he said, closing his eyes.

But he wasn't.

It was just too hot!

"I need to find a way to cool down," Bat said.

He flapped out of the roost and up to a high branch near the top of the beech tree. There, he hung upside down, trying to catch a breeze on his warm fur. But barely a leaf stirred.

"Right then," he said. "I'll make my own wind."

He waved his wings forwards and backwards, backwards and forwards, fanning air over his body. The breeze felt wonderful and soon he was a little cooler.

"That'll do it," he said. "Now I'll fall straight back to sleep."

But it was no good.

It was still too hot!

Bat felt ready to burst, he was so full up with hot air! He wished he could pant like Wolf, roll in the mud like Wild Boar or sweat like Bear… He had no way of cooling down. He'd have to leave his favourite roosting tree and find another way to escape the heat. Perhaps he'd seek out a chilly cave or flap through the icy spray of a waterfall.

Bat wasn't best pleased about the idea of flying in the daytime but there was nothing else for it. He launched off from the beech branch and swooped further into the forest, seeking something that might help him to cool down. He flew between leafy branches, squinting in the sunlight. His eyes weren't used to the blinding brightness.

"Bat, is that you?" called a voice. Bat saw Squirrel at the base of an oak tree. She scampered up the trunk to get a better look at him as he came close. "I'm surprised to see you out! It's a lovely day, isn't it?"

"No, not really," said Bat, and carried on through the trees.

The sun blazed above, warming the back of Bat's wings as he flew on. He kept a lookout for a cave or waterfall. In a clearing filled with sunny dandelions, Bat could smell Rabbit. She was lying in the grass and munching on some leaves.

"Hello, Bat!" she said when she spotted him. "Enjoying the sunshine?"

"Definitely not," said Bat, darting through the clearing and swooping back under the cover of the trees. His wings felt heavy, like they were trying to flap through hot mud rather than hot air. Everything looked unfamiliar in the light and he couldn't spot a cave anywhere. Normally Bat used his special hearing to work out where he was going, listening to echoes to steer through the trees. But the forest was so loud in the daytime! He could hardly hear himself think over the birdsong and animal chatter. Even the roaring river seemed louder somehow…

"Hello, Bat," said Duck, bobbing in the water. "It's odd to see you out! Fancied a flap in the daytime, did you?"

"No, I didn't," Bat snapped. "The forest is far too hot – not to mention noisy and crowded."

"It's not too hot for me here," said Duck, fluffing up his feathers. "The cool water stops me overheating."

Bat pulled up short, gazing at the glittering river. A quick dip would be a brilliant way to cool down.

"Watch out!" Bat called to Duck. He plunged towards the river. Just as he was about to hit the water, Bat pulled out of his dive and skimmed the surface, soaking his belly, and spraying Duck with a huge splash. The cool water clung to his fur. It was fantastically refreshing!

"Thanks for the tip!" cried Bat as he flapped away.

"No problem!" replied Duck.

Bat tucked his head against his fur and licked up a few droplets of wonderful water. That was so much better. His wings light and limber once more, Bat flew back home.

"Hello again, Bat," said Rabbit, still munching dandelions in the clearing.

"Goodbye again, Rabbit," said Bat, as he whizzed past. He had somewhere to be!

Beside the oak tree, Squirrel's fluffy tail flicked as she watched Bat flash by. "Hopefully see you soon!" she called.

"Hopefully not!" said Bat. He didn't plan on waking up in the daytime ever again.

When Bat next woke, all was peaceful. He peered out of his hollow to see a shadowy, silver forest. The moon shone in the sky and a gentle breeze tickled his fur.

He swung out of his roost and flapped off into the cool, quiet night. Bat sent high sharp cries out into the darkness and the noises bounced back. It was his special way of mapping out the forest. From the different sounds, Bat could tell how big objects were, and how far away.

"This is much more like it," said Bat, as he swooped on through the trees, flying deeper and deeper into the still, night-time forest.

"I snooze in the day and soar through the night,
When the air is cool, and the moon is bright.
My eyesight's not bad, my smell's pretty good,
But hearing is best for exploring the wood."

Beyond Tadpole's Pond

Tadpole looked at the lumpy, bumpy thing poking out of her side. What could it be? She wriggled through the water, searching for somebody to ask. She spotted one of her brothers munching on the wavy green weeds and darted over to him.

"Look!" Tadpole said, using her tail to point at the lump. "What do you think this is?"

As her brother swam closer Tadpole spotted a lump on his side, just like hers. "Oh, you've got one too!" Tadpole said. "No, wait, you've got two of them."

There was one on his other side as well!

"They're just legs," said her brother. "We're turning into big green frogs. Soon we'll hop, hop, hop out of the pond."

"But I don't want legs," said Tadpole. "And I don't want to hop out of the pond. I want to stay swimming in here forever."

"Don't worry," said her brother. "Legs are great for swimming – watch!"

He flicked his little legs and paddled through the water. But Tadpole wasn't convinced.

"I have a tail," she said. "I can swim just as well with that." And off she squiggled.

Over the next few days, Tadpole grew one, two, three and then four legs. While her siblings got excited about the idea of life beyond the pond, Tadpole tried to ignore the strange changes. But soon her tail began to shrink and Tadpole had to use her new legs to paddle.

One by one her brothers and sisters transformed into frogs, rose to the surface and slipped out of the water. Had they disappeared forever? Soon she was the last tadpole in the pond.

Plink! Tadpole looked up as a cluster of tiny orbs plopped into the water above her. A fully grown frog splashed into the pond beside them. Tadpole swam up to take a closer look and she spotted squirming black specks inside each orb.

"What are they?" she asked the frog.

"These are my eggs," the frog replied. "You used to look just like this. Then you became a squiggly tadpole and now you're a little frog!"

Tadpole looked at her stretchy legs and webbed feet and saw that it was true! She had become a frog whether she wanted to or not. But that got her thinking – when she was a squiggly black speck she didn't know there was a whole pond out here. She had thought her little egg was the whole world…

Maybe she should just take a quick peek out of the pond.

Frog took a big brave breath, swam to the surface and splashed through it. Her brothers and sisters hadn't disappeared! Some of them were gathered on the bank or sitting on glossy lily pads. Beyond the sparkling pool, copper trees stood straight and tall, their branches reaching out to tickle each other with bushy leaves. Frog paddled to the water's edge and launched herself on to the bank. Her springy legs felt strong!

"This isn't scary at all," said Frog. "Hopping feels fantastic! In fact, I think I'll hop, hop, hop off and explore the forest."

"Now that I'm a frog, I can jump and swim,
I can breathe out of water, and within!
I'll hop off to find a new place to stay,
Then return here to lay my eggs someday."

AUTUMN

THE BEAVERS' BIG BUILD

"Can you hear that, Kit?" asked Daddy Beaver.

Kit listened hard. He *could* hear something. A strange trickling, tinkling sound outside their lodge, the mound of sticks they called home.

"It sounds like running water!" Kit said.

"That's right," said Daddy Beaver. "Come with me."

Daddy Beaver dived into the water. Kit followed, swimming through the underwater channel out into the pond. The beavers surfaced and looked around.

"There," said Daddy Beaver. "I knew it! There's a crack in the dam."

The beavers' dam ran across the width of the pool, made of tightly packed wood, stones and soil. Sure enough, Kit spotted water gushing through a gap where the twigs had been washed away. The heavy rain from the night before must have caused the damage.

"We need to fix it," said Daddy Beaver. "I think there's another storm coming and we can't risk the hole getting bigger."

Kit looked at the puffy purple clouds hanging in the sky. A storm certainly seemed to be on its way…

"I need your help, Kit," said Daddy Beaver. "We have to collect more wood as quickly as we can."

"From the forest?" asked Kit worriedly. Their pond had flooded the surrounding woodland, creating useful channels for the beavers to swim along. But Kit didn't like going under the gloomy trees.

"It's important that we fix the dam," said Daddy Beaver, giving Kit a gentle nudge. "Without it, this pond will disappear. Then where would we build our lodge? This safe spot protects us from predators. Come on, I'll be with you every splash of the way."

Kit took a deep breath and tried to feel brave. He paddled through the water with his webbed feet, using his wide tail to steer, and followed Daddy Beaver down a narrow channel. The sky disappeared as they dipped beneath the trees. A twig snapped nearby and Kit slapped his tail in fright.

"It was only a squirrel, Kit," Daddy Beaver reassured him. "Don't worry – if something scary comes along, we'll dip back under the water and head for our lodge. OK?"

"OK," said Kit. But he wasn't so sure.

"Here!" said Daddy Beaver, swimming over to a large branch on the bank. "Why don't you take that one?"

"It looks a bit big for me. I won't be able to get it back," said Kit doubtfully.

"Trust me," said Daddy Beaver. "You'll be fine. First we gnaw off the bark, like this..."

He began chewing away at the flaky outer layer of the log. Kit splashed over and together the two beavers gnawed. The wood was tasty! Before long they'd stripped the branch. With Daddy Beaver's help, Kit gripped the log between his teeth and began swimming back towards the dam. Daddy Beaver was right – it was easy to tug it through the water! Kit quickly reached the dam. He clambered on to it, heaving the log into place to fill the gap.

"Well done, Kit!" said Daddy Beaver, swimming up behind him with a log of his own. "Now take some of that mossy mud from the bank, to make sure the stick stays secure."

Kit collected the mud, cupping it with his paws, and packed the log in tightly. The two beavers headed back into the forest. Kit barely noticed the spooky shadows this time. He was too busy hunting for useful bits of wood.

It wasn't long before the dam was fixed and the sound of trickling water had disappeared. This was turning out to be quite fun!

"Shall we patch up the lodge too?" asked Kit. "Just in case it's a very bad storm."

"Excellent idea!" said Daddy Beaver. "We don't want the roof to fall in."

Once again the beavers made their way into the forest, returning with mouthfuls of sticks. They clambered on top of the mound of wood, packing in the sticks to fill any gaps that might let water into their lodge.

The sky roared with thunder and chilly rain began to fall. Daddy Beaver and Kit dived into the pond, slipping along the tunnel into their lodge.

"Thank you for helping today, Kit," said Daddy Beaver. "You're going to make an excellent builder."

The beavers snuggled up beside each other and fell asleep to the muffled rumbles of thunder overhead.

The next morning the storm had dwindled to a dreary drizzle. The two beavers swam out into the pond.

"Oh no!" said Kit.

"What's wrong?" asked Daddy Beaver.

"There's not a crack in sight!" said Kit with a sigh. "Yesterday was brilliant. I wanted to patch up the dam again today."

Daddy Beaver chuckled. "We'll need to fix our home again soon enough."

Kit somersaulted in excitement. He couldn't wait to put his building skills to the test once more!

"Our dam stayed strong through the stormy night,
But if it cracks again, we'll be all right,
Now that little Kit knows the perfect fix,
He'll patch it up with stones, mud and sticks!"

MOLE AND THE MISSING WORM

Buried beneath a muddy bank at the forest's edge, Mole was busily going about his business. The only sign that he was there was a small mound of mud at the entrance to his hole.

"Where on earth did I leave my lunch?" Mole muttered to himself.

He scurried along a tunnel and into the chamber at the end. Somewhere within his maze-like home was a fresh, juicy earthworm, just waiting to be eaten. It had fallen through the top of a tunnel this morning and Mole had felt the tell-tale thud as it hit the ground. He'd scampered around until he found it, then had given the worm a powerful paralyzing bite to stop it from wriggling off. Mole had stored it in one of his many chambers to save it for later. Now his tummy was rumbling, but the earthworm was nowhere to be found.

"It's got to be around here somewhere," he said, sniffing the air to try to catch its scent. Yes, he could smell it nearby! Mole set off once again. He clambered from tunnel to tunnel. Where could it be? His impressive underground network spread far and wide. The walls were crisscrossed with roots, leading up to the tall trees and smaller shrubs above the surface.

Hardly any light made it into Mole's magnificent home, but he didn't need to see to get around. His whiskers tickled the tunnels' edges and helped him to tell where he was going. His spade-like hands scooped the soil out of the way as he went along and his nose sniffed out any tasty food or hidden dangers that might be lurking nearby.

As he rounded the corner into one of his new tunnels he came to an abrupt stop. Heavy rain the night before had shaken and stirred the soil. Now the whole soggy lot seemed to have fallen down into the tunnel, blocking Mole from going any further.

"Bother! I'll have to fix this before I find that worm," said Mole.

He shovelled away at the soil, pushing his paws in wide circles like he was swimming through the mud. He worked quickly, patting the earth into the sides of the tunnel until everything was neat and tidy. That was better!

Mole scurried the rest of the way along the tunnel, checking for any more mishaps. But the passage was clear.

"Still, this tunnel does feel rather short," Mole said when he reached a dead end. "Wouldn't it be nice if it went on a bit further?"

A longer tunnel would mean even more earthworms falling in…

Mole pondered this for a moment. Lunch could wait.

Once again, Mole began to dig. He scraped away at the soil. Soon he had dug a long, winding tunnel, wide enough for his furry body to scamper along. He pushed the loose earth up to the surface, making another muddy hump above ground.

Mole placed his paws on the molehill and pulled himself up. He stuck his nose out and sniffed the world above. A chilly wind whisked by, carrying the sharp scent of fresh rain.

"Why would anybody want to live above ground?" he wondered.

The weather was always changing – too hot one minute and too cold the next! Beneath the soil things stayed constantly cosy. Better yet, food dropped into your lap! Talking of which, Mole's nose twitched as he caught a whiff of something yummy. The worm! It was close.

Mole scurried back underground, sniffing as hard as he could, his super sensitive nose twitching and trembling to try to work out where it was.

Mole crawled round corners, bumped along bends and wriggled through tunnels until…

There it was!

Just where he'd left it, of course.

Mole munched on the earthworm – it was as juicy and delicious as he'd hoped.

Full up from his meal, and with his paws aching from all that digging, Mole suddenly felt very sleepy.

"I think I'll go and have a nap," he said. He whipped along the tunnel all the way to his nest, the soil slipping over his velvety fur. Curling up in his grotto full of spongy dead leaves, Mole drifted off. He hoped there would be another juicy worm waiting for him when he woke up!

"Burrower and builder, I live below ground,
In a maze of tunnels, marked with a mound.
With my earth-moving paws, I like to roam.
This shadowy soil world is home, sweet home."

Mouse's Secret House

Mouse tugged another straw of hay towards her nest and tucked it in neatly. Her little ball-shaped home was nearly finished, hidden away in the long grass. The nest was lined with squishy leaves, spongy moss and bits of fluff. It was the perfect place to take cover from the cold weather that was on its way, and to keep her safe from enemies!

"It looks ever so cosy in there," she said proudly. "But I wonder if I could make it even cosier..."

She leaped from her nest on to a bendy blade of grass, wrapping her toes round the stem and holding her tail out for balance. She jumped again and landed on the top of a dandelion clock, sending seeds whizzing into the sky. Mouse peered around the meadow, searching for something that might make a squishy, squashy, spongy addition to her nest.

"What's that?" exclaimed Mouse, spotting something fuzzy waving in the wind near the trees at the edge of the forest. It was a feather! That would be perfect!

Mouse hopped down, scampering along the ground towards the feather. Soon the trees towered over her. To Mouse they looked like they were propping up the sky. As she got closer, the feather grew larger and larger. When she reached it, it was almost three times her length!

"It's a little bigger than I expected," said Mouse. "But bigger is better! And it does look very comfy."

It had black-and-brown stripes with small flecks of gold, and a white fluffy bit at the bottom. She nipped the tip of the feather between her teeth and began scurrying back to her nest. It was much harder to see where she was going with the big feather to carry!

"Ooooh!" cried a voice above. "What have you found, Mouse?"

Mouse looked up. Squirrel was peering down from a hollow in a tree, her paws wrapped round a shiny acorn.

"That's a nice feather!" Squirrel called. "Can I have it for my drey?"

"No," said Mouse, with the feather still firmly between her teeth. "It's mine!"

With an indignant squeak, Squirrel darted back inside her home. Mouse barely had time to take another step before she heard somebody else calling from up above.

"Kek! Kek!" It was Woodpecker, perched on a bare branch. "I'd love that beautiful feather for my hole. Can I have it?"

"No," Mouse mumbled, turning her back. "It's mine!"

Mouse didn't stick around. She darted into the long grass of the meadow, determined to get away from the nosy woodland creatures.

"They should go and search for their own feather if they want one so badly," she said. This special, gold-flecked feather was hers!

Suddenly Vole nipped out of his hidden nest, making Mouse jump and drop the feather.

"Hello!" said Vole. "I thought I heard somebody."

"Hello there," said Mouse, scuttling in front of her prize to hide it from Vole's curious eyes. But Vole had already spotted it.

"Oh, I like your feather!" he said, darting around Mouse to get a better look. "Please can I borrow it for my burrow?"

"No!" said Mouse, snatching it up with her paws. "It is absolutely, completely, definitely mine and NOBODY ELSE IS HAVING IT!"

"Actually," said a voice behind her. "I think you'll find it's mine."

Vole darted back into his underground burrow. Mouse turned round, her heart thump-thump-thumping. She took in the terrifying creature…

Thick talons with sharp black claws.

Yellow eyes, fixed hungrily on her.

Black-and-brown striped feathers, flecked with gold.

It was Hawk!

That was very bad news.

With a panicked squeak, Mouse left the feather where it lay and dashed into the long grass. She heard Hawk's sharp beak snap and whipped her tail out of the way just in time! She rushed through the grass, listening out for the flap of powerful wings. Finally she spotted her nest. Mouse leaped inside, shaking. That was a close one! Thankfully Hawk would never find her in this well-hidden home.

"On second thoughts, it's cosy enough in here already," said Mouse, curling up into a little ball. "I didn't need that feather anyway…"

"The world's a scary place for a little mouse,
But I feel safe inside my secret house.
Here I'm hidden away from beady eyes,
There's no way hungry Hawk will spot me inside!"

The Ladybird Huddle

A chilly breeze whooshed through the woods. It shook the last of the leaves from their branches and left a trail of silver frost across the forest. Perched on a blade of grass, Ladybird felt the change in the wind and sensed winter was on its way. Her six legs tingled, as if itching to be off somewhere. "Fly up high, Ladybird!" the wind seemed to whisper.

Ladybird hadn't felt anything like it before. She'd never wanted to go further than this little forest clearing, let alone into the great unknown. But her legs kept tingling and her antennae were tickling, and she decided it was time to listen to her instincts.

With a last look around the clearing, she took off. Her wings whirred as she rose higher and higher, leaving the forest floor behind. The fallen leaves below became an amber blur as she reached the first branches of the trees…

Uh-oh! Who was that, dangling down from a delicate web?

Spider swung on the end of a silk thread, watching to see if the little red beetle was going to get stuck.

"Oh dear!" said Ladybird. "I don't want to get caught in her sticky web."

She put on a burst of speed...

Whizz! Zoom! Zip! She rocketed through, tearing a hole in Spider's home.

"Sorry, Spider," she called back. "I'm too speedy to get stuck!"

Ladybird wiped her feet together to clean off the sticky strands and flew on. She rose up through the almost-bare branches, wondering where she was going to end up...

Uh-oh! Who was that, tapping her beak on a hollow tree? Woodpecker pecked and poked, searching for insects beneath the bark.

"Oh dear!" said Ladybird. "I don't want to be Woodpecker's supper."

The bird's head whipped up. Her sharp eyes followed Ladybird as she flitted past. Ladybird fanned out her wing cases, showing off her bright red-and-black markings.

"Urgh!" said Woodpecker. "You look poisonous. I bet I'd get tummy trouble if I ate you."

Ladybird's special spots had saved her from becoming the bird's snack!

Up Ladybird flew, until she'd cleared the branches. Above her, the wide, open sky darkened to a dusky blue. Clouds rushed across it, hurried along by the gusty winds. Ladybird had been flying for almost an hour! But she had a feeling she wouldn't have to keep going for much longer...

Suddenly the wind whisked beneath her wings, tugging her towards a steep mountain. It grew closer and closer, looming over Ladybird, until she was being swept along the tops of the trees lining its slopes, towards the summit. Eventually the wind ran out of puff and set Ladybird down on the thin branch of a silver birch tree.

Ladybird looked around. Up here, the forest was thinner than down in the valley. Tall, narrow pines stretched up to the clouds, their needles scattered across the floor. Ladybird spotted a hollow log covered in strange red patches. "I'm miles from home," she said. "But I've got a feeling that this is exactly where I'm meant to be."

There was a faint funny scent that seemed to get stronger as Ladybird scuttled along the branch.

"It smells just like me!" exclaimed Ladybird.

Beetles from long ago had left a trail, marking a secret path along the branch with their scent. The trail led Ladybird down the side of the tree to the leafy ground...

Uh-oh! Who was that, swooping down from his roost?

Bat flapped his great grey wings and launched himself towards Ladybird.

"Oh dear!" said Ladybird. "I don't want to become a snack for Bat!"

She froze as Bat swooped towards her. Luckily she had one last trick. She squeezed out smelly yellow goo from her knees.

"Yuck! You stink!" said Bat, getting a whiff of the goo. "There must be something wrong with this bug."

He flapped his wings and launched back into the air. Ladybird's special defences had saved her once more!

Ladybird began to scuttle along the scent trail again. As she scrambled over the sticks and stones she was joined by other ladybirds, all heading in the same direction as her.

"Do you know where we're going?" Ladybird asked.

"No idea," said another beetle. "I've never been here in my life. But this feels like the right way, doesn't it?"

They arrived at the hollow log and an amazing sight greeted them. Thousands of beetles were clambering over each other, creating wriggling red patches that covered the wood! Inside there were even more squiggling beetles.

"What are you all doing?" asked Ladybird, climbing into the log.

"We're settling in for the winter!" somebody replied.

Of course! Snuggled inside this log, the ladybirds could

huddle up and snooze through the chilly months.

"I think I'll join you," Ladybird said, scrambling in.

Right at the top of the log, Ladybird found herself a good spot, squished in with hundreds of others. Gradually the beetles settled down and fell asleep.

Outside the howling wind picked up. Over the following months, it drove showers of freezing rain through the woods. But inside the hollow log, Ladybird was snug.

Finally the icy winds moved on and spots of green appeared on the branches. The clouds parted and the sun peeked down once more. Ladybird woke up as its pale rays filled the log with light.

She opened her spotted wing cases and stretched her wings. They quivered, ready to fly.

"Goodbye!" Ladybird called to her sleepy companions. "Thanks for the winter huddle!"

She launched off from the log, out into the wood where the new greenery was bright and welcoming.

"I've added my smell to the scent trail here,
So new ladybirds can find their way next year.
My spots say 'danger!', my knees squeeze out goo –
I wouldn't eat me if I were you!"

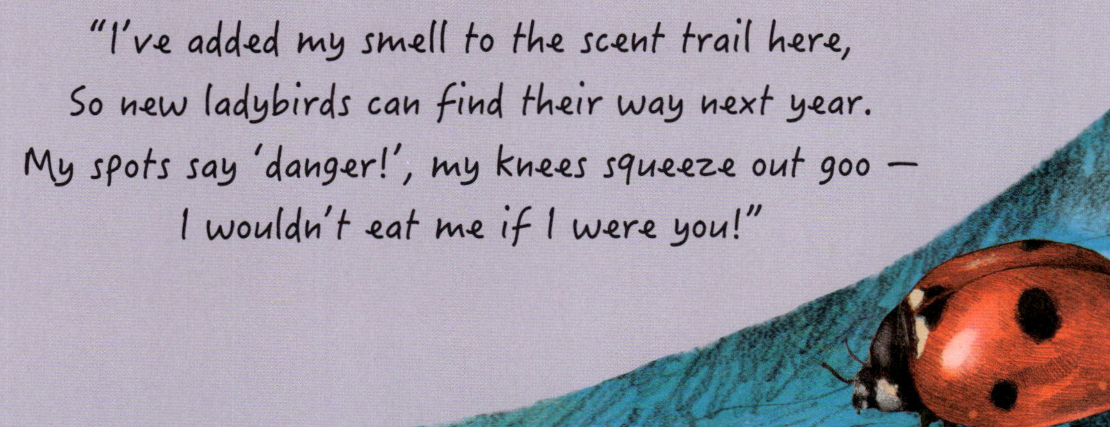

Fawn's Lost Spots

Fawn peered into the pool. He stretched his neck this way and that, checking every part of his body from his spindly legs to his fluffy tummy. Where had all his spots gone? He had been dotted with hundreds of white flecks not long ago and now there wasn't a single spot to be seen!

"They can't have gone far..." said the little deer to himself.

He glanced back at his cosy bed – a circle of squashy, spongy grass. Mummy Hind would be back to check on him soon. She'd left him in this safe spot, tucked out of sight, earlier that afternoon. But it wouldn't take long to have a quick look around for his spots...

Fawn set off through the towering trees. A chilly breeze made the branches dance and brown leaves fluttered to the floor. He stopped in front of a fat red toadstool.

"Maybe these are my spots," said Fawn, nudging the toadstool with his hoof. But the toadstool's spots were too small and yellowy.

Fawn carried on until he reached a tree twisted with honeysuckle. His ears pricked at the whir of wings. A beautiful black-and-white butterfly settled on a flower.

"Excuse me," said Fawn. "Have you borrowed my spots?"

The butterfly shot up into the sky. As she opened her wings, Fawn saw her white spots were too big and splodgy. He set off again.

The night drew in. Gloomy shadows spread. Puddles of silver moonlight dappled the floor.

"Oh dear, it's late," said Fawn. "Mummy Hind will be wondering where I am. I should get back."

The leaves crunched under Fawn's hooves as he trotted back to the pool. But when he reached it, Fawn bleated in surprise. Hundreds of white flecks were floating in the water. He had found his spots! Now he just had to get them out…

Fawn jammed his hooves into the mud and leaned forwards. He stretched closer and closer, until his nose was nuzzling the surface.

"Fawn?" called Mummy Hind.

Fawn jumped. His hooves skidded and slipped on the slimy mud until…

SPLASH! He toppled into the water.

Fawn shook his head as droplets dribbled off his nose and ears. Mummy Hind fished out her soggy son and licked his fur clean.

"Where have you been, little one?" she asked. "I was so worried about you!"

"I've been looking for my spots," said Fawn. "They're in the pool. See?"

Mummy Hind looked into the water. "Those spots are the stars' reflections," she said, rubbing her nose against his cheek.

"Oh," said Fawn, puzzled. He looked up at the sky through the canopy of leaves. Hundreds of stars twinkled above. "Where have my spots gone then?"

Mummy Hind led Fawn back to his bed. He curled up like a fern leaf, tucking his nose to his tummy.

"You don't need your spots any more," Mummy Hind said. "When you were tiny, they helped you to blend in with the forest floor so it was difficult for dangerous creatures to see you. But now you're stronger, you can protect yourself.

And as you've been getting stronger, your fur has grown out and your spots have disappeared. Soon you'll be one of the biggest animals in the forest!"

"I will?" asked Fawn sleepily.

"You will," said Mummy Hind. "And you'll grow grand antlers each year like Daddy Stag."

"Wow!" said Fawn, thinking of the amazing crown of antlers Daddy Stag wore so proudly. "When will they grow?"

"Once the green comes again," said Mummy Hind. "Now sleep, little one."

Soon the fiery reds and oranges of autumn gave way to the greys and browns of winter. Eventually the sun warmed the forest floor enough that tiny bursts of green began to appear. Now Fawn was bigger, he began to search for his favourite foods alone, tasty tough bracken and pine roots.

One morning in early spring, Fawn came across a pond. As he peered into the water he saw two hard points sticking out between his ears, like new tree shoots.

"My antlers!" he said. They weren't much yet

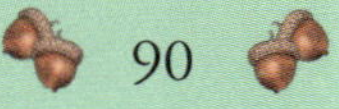

but one day they would be as big as Daddy Stag's! Fawn hardly recognized the deer staring back at him. He'd changed so much since that autumn night when he'd mistaken the stars for his lost spots.

"My spots have vanished, now my antlers grow,
They'll fall to the ground before the first snow.
When the green comes again, they'll reappear,
A year of big changes for a little deer!"

WINTER

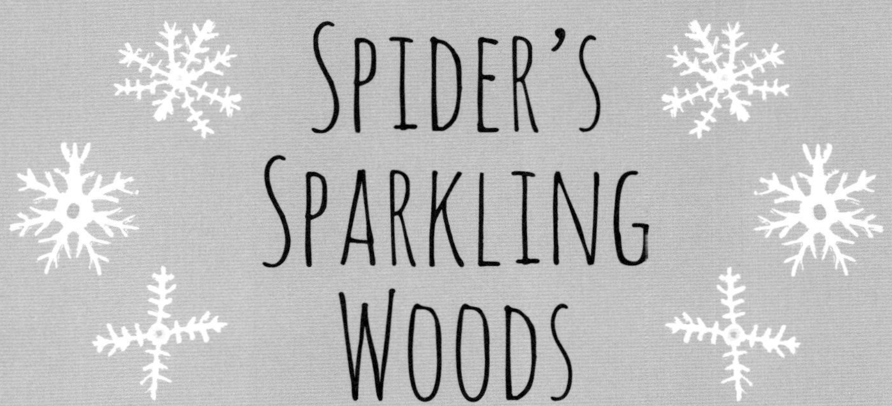

Spider's Sparkling Woods

A golden, star-shaped leaf tugged away from the topmost branch of a horse chestnut tree and floated down to the forest floor. It settled on top of the other amber, brown and scarlet leaves coating the ground.

Hidden among them, Spider was speedily spinning. Earlier that morning she had laid a pouch of tiny eggs. Now she needed to make sure her little ones would be cosy enough to survive the winter.

So Spider spun. She wove threads round and round, her eight legs working together to wrap the pouch in a springy silk cloud. When she had finished, she looked around for the perfect place to put it.

"That star-shaped leaf looks special enough for my eggs," she said, hurrying over to it, tightly clutching the little pouch.

She spun some more sticky threads and stuck the pouch to the underside of the golden leaf, safe from the cold and from the beady eyes of enemies.

She checked the pouch one last time, squeezing together any threads that showed signs of unravelling.

"Stay snug!" she whispered.

Spider scuttled away, clambering over spiky green cases, some cracked, revealing the smooth conkers hidden within. She soon reached her web and climbed up to her favourite spot, right in the centre. In only a few weeks' time she would need to find somewhere snug to bed down for the cold months herself. She'd better eat as many flies as she could in the meantime!

Days passed and the winds picked up, making the silk threads of her web quiver. When the first frosts came, Spider knew it was time to find a warm place to spend the winter. Once again she scurried across the forest floor. When she passed the star-shaped leaf, she couldn't resist taking a peek. The pouch was still securely stuck underneath.

"I wonder whether my little ones have hatched yet," she said. It was impossible to tell from the outside. The tiny spider siblings would spend the winter huddled up together within the pouch before emerging in the spring.

Spider crawled up the side of the chestnut tree until she found a hollow space behind a peeling piece of bark. Tucking into it, Spider spun a silk pocket round herself. When the pod was almost complete, she took a last look out at the forest. Far below she could see her web, glittering with frost. It looked like a snowflake suspended in the air.

In the spring her little ones would set off into the woods, spinning their shimmering homes across this part of the forest. She couldn't wait to see their handiwork!

"When spring comes, my young leave their eggs,
Scuttle into the forest to stretch their legs.
They'll weave silk strands, through day and night
Their own fine webs that catch the light."

Wolf All Alone

Black Wolf woke up as the sun was sinking. Snowflakes were settling on his nose. He could feel the pack shifting and shuffling around him.

"Come on, sleepyhead," said Alpha, nudging his paw. "It's time to go!"

Black Wolf got to his feet and gave his shaggy head a shake. At only three years old, he was one of the youngest wolves in the pack.

"Tonight we're going on a journey to stretch our territory," Alpha told the wolves. "We'll head east through the forest."

"Can we go west instead?" Black Wolf asked, staring across the valley. In the dimming light he could make out a line of tree-covered mountains, rising in great green waves.

He'd always wondered what lay beyond them.

"No," said Alpha. "We're going east, and that's that."

Black Wolf didn't like being ignored, but Alpha usually knew best. They set off through the thick blanket of snow, forming a winding river of wolves with Alpha keeping watch at the rear. Black Wolf kept glancing back at the mysterious mountains, getting smaller and smaller until he could only just see their peaks spearing the sky. The white moon rose and fell as the wolves trudged on.

"Stop!" said Alpha. "We'll rest here."

The pack drew to a halt. Black Wolf bumped into the wolf in front of him.

"Watch out!" she said.

"Sorry," said Black Wolf. He leaped over to Alpha. "I'm not tired yet. Can we keep going for a bit?"

"No," said Alpha. "We're resting here, and that's that."

That was twice he'd been ignored! Black Wolf slunk away and didn't speak out again. They had stretched their territory a little further, and some of the older wolves had hunted down dinner for the pack.

I suppose it's been a good night, Black Wolf thought to himself as he settled down to sleep. So why did he feel so unhappy?

Alpha was a brilliant leader – he kept the pack warm and fed and looked out for the littlest members. But Black

Wolf wanted more than food and protection. He wanted to be listened to. And he wanted adventure! Black Wolf tossed and turned – what should he do? By the time the wolves gathered again at dusk, he'd made a big decision.

Soon after sunset, the wolves got into line. All of them, except Black Wolf.

"I'm setting off on my own," he told the pack. He glanced back, peering through the falling snow. "I want to see what's beyond those mountains."

Alpha tossed his mighty head and stepped forwards. "Good for you," he said, nuzzling Black Wolf. "I thought you might leave us one day to make your own way. But being a lone wolf is tough. You'll need to be brave, young one."

Black Wolf licked Alpha's cheek. "Thank you for everything you've taught me."

"Good luck!" called the pack. "We'll miss you!"

With a farewell howl, Black Wolf turned and set out towards the wild western mountains. This was it! He was off on his own adventure!

He walked for miles and miles. At first he bounded along, with a feeling of excitement, but before long he slowed to a plod. In the pack, the wolves at the front swept the snow aside with their strides, clearing the way for those behind them. Now he had to do all the work on his own. The snow drifted down steadily.

As the sun rose over the faraway mountains, the forest was flooded with rays of red and orange. The fiery colours filled Black Wolf with courage. As the morning wore on, he bedded down beneath a huge fir tree. Curling up as tight as he could, Black Wolf tucked his nose to his tail. But even his thick fur couldn't keep out the cold. Without the rest of the pack to cuddle up to, he shivered and shook.

The days slipped by and the mountains grew closer. Though he was still excited to see what he'd find beyond them, journeying alone had been much harder than Black Wolf had expected. Hunting without a pack was almost

impossible and he often had to go without any food. Long, cold days slipped into lonely nights.

Finally all that separated him from the mountains' foothills was a whooshing river. He'd almost made it! Black Wolf plunged in. He paddled through the freezing water and splashed on to the bank.

Seven shadows skulked out of the trees. It was another wolf pack! They prowled towards him, their coats gleaming in the evening sun. Their leader paced forwards, towering over Black Wolf.

"This is our land," said the great grey wolf. "You need to leave. Now!"

SNAP! The wolf lunged towards Black Wolf's leg and slammed his sharp teeth together, trying to bite him. Black Wolf darted out of the way just in time and began to run.

"Be brave!" he told himself as the pack snarled and snapped behind him. He ran alongside the river, uphill. Up and up and up he went, the snow crumbling beneath his paws as he followed the winding water through the forest. Every time a tree crackled or creaked, he jumped. He felt like danger was everywhere! He wished there was someone to watch his back.

When Black Wolf finally stopped running, the great grey wolf's territory was far behind. He had almost reached the top of the mountains! Though he was exhausted, Black Wolf pushed on. He was so close to seeing what lay beyond the soaring peaks. He scrambled over the rocky slopes, up to the very top, and peered down at the world below. The thick, bumpy blanket of trees was dotted with frozen lakes and glittering waterfalls, snow-covered cliffs and sloping craters. And it was all his to explore.

"Still," Black Wolf said sadly. "I would have liked to share it with someone."

He sat on the mountain top as the moon rose. A long, lonely howl bubbled up inside him. He sang a song of sorrow to the sky.

HAAA-WOOO!

A reply rang out in the darkness!

HAAA-WOOO! HAAA-WOOO!

Black Wolf listened to the other wolf's answering howl. She didn't sound unfriendly. She sounded lonely too – and close!

He hurried down the other side of the mountain, towards the new wolf's haunting howls. He found her in a clearing, her fur as white as the full moon above.

"I've been waiting for you," White Wolf said. "Would you like to join my pack?"

Black Wolf wavered. He didn't want to get bossed around

in a pack again. He'd spent too long on his own to go back to being ignored.

"How many wolves are in your pack?" he asked.

"If you join," said White Wolf, "there'll be two of us."

Black Wolf barked with joy – a pack of his very own! Together he and White Wolf could discover the mysteries of the mountains and never be lonely again. In these wild woods, two was much better than one.

They curled up beside each other, warm and cosy, and fell fast asleep. They slept all day, waking as the sun sank towards the horizon. Far below, an icy emerald lake glittered in the twilight.

"Let's explore that lake tonight," said Black Wolf.

"Good idea," said White Wolf. "You lead the way. I've got your back."

Black Wolf yipped with happiness – his adventures had only just begun!

"I left my pack behind, walked far from home,
And discovered it's tough to live on your own.
I howled to the sky and White Wolf replied,
I can't wait to explore, with her by my side."

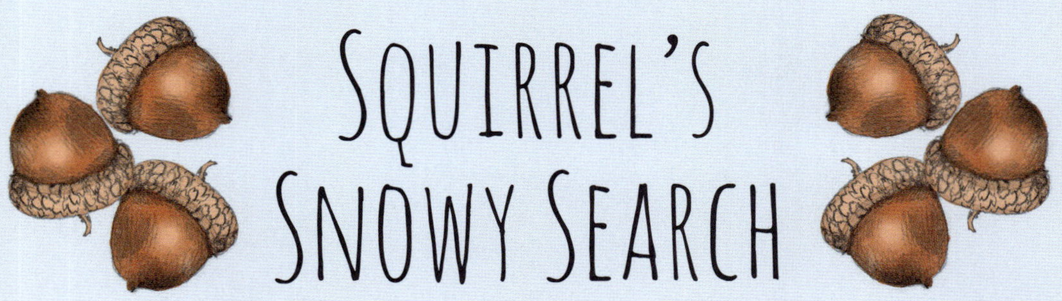

Squirrel's Snowy Search

Squirrel stuck her nose out of the drey. A cold snowflake settled on it, making her whiskers twitch. Beneath her a glittering white blanket covered the forest floor.

Now that the bright berries and lush leaves of summer had disappeared, lots of animals didn't have enough to eat. They had fallen into a deep sleep for the winter and would wake up again when the food returned. The bears were snoozing in their caves, the hedgehogs were huddled in their leaf piles, and even the beetles and spiders had found somewhere warm to bed down for the winter. But Squirrel didn't need to sleep through the cold months. Food may be scarce in the forest but she had planned ahead.

Back in the autumn, Squirrel had hunted high and low for nuts to hoard. And not just any old nuts. Squirrel was very picky! First, she'd sniffed each one to see if it was rotten, then she'd examined it closely for cracks and finally she'd given it a good shake to check there was a tasty seed inside. Only nuts that had passed Squirrel's tough tests made it into her collection. Day after day, as the leaves had faded and fluttered to the ground, Squirrel had dug little holes and hidden her nuts away beneath the soil.

Now the forest was transformed into a winter wonderland, without an acorn or hazelnut in sight. "It's a good job I'm so well prepared," said Squirrel. "Though it might be trickier to find those nuts with everything covered in snow."

Luckily she had an excellent memory where food was concerned! Squirrel scampered out of her drey on to the trunk then leaped on to the neighbouring tree. She flew from branch to branch, sending clumps of snow crashing to the floor below. Suddenly Squirrel stopped jumping. This clearing definitely looked familiar...

"Aha! I remember that holly bush with its brilliant red berries," she said, climbing down the tree and bounding over, her bushy tail swishing. She pressed her nose to the ground and smelled a sweet, nutty scent. "I'm sure my hazelnut collection is buried right here." Squirrel had grouped all her different types of nuts together so that she had a better chance of recalling where she'd hidden them.

But she didn't fancy hazelnuts today.

Squirrel scampered on, searching for more landmarks that matched the map of the forest in her head. There was the shrub shaped like a mushroom, its leaves now sagging with snow. There was the shallow pond, its frozen surface mirroring the pale sky above. Squirrel had a feeling that her hoard of big, juicy acorns was very close.

Beside the pond, Squirrel caught the earthy scent of her favourite food and began to dig. Her little paws whirred as she chipped away at the soil that was stiff with frost. Finally her claws struck the smooth, shiny shell of an acorn and she pulled her prize out of the ground.

"Hello, lovely acorn," said Squirrel. She bit through the tough shell to get to the tasty seed inside. It was good to know that she had hundreds more of these hidden beneath the forest. Thanks to her secret stash, Squirrel would not go hungry this winter.

"Each autumn I hide all the nuts that I can,
So when winter comes I have a feeding plan!
If I forget an acorn buried deep below,
From that lost nut, a new oak tree will grow."

FOX FOLLOWS HIS FEET

"Wake up, Pup!"

Pup's ears pricked and he opened one bleary eye. His sister's nose was pressed against his.

"There's something you have to see," said his sister. "Come on!"

Pup followed her out of the den, slipping under the crooked roots at the entrance. His nose stung as they emerged into the evening forest. But it was a forest Pup had never seen before!

Every branch, shrub and boulder was covered in a layer of glittering white. The bumpy floor had been transformed into a smooth, shimmering carpet. Mummy Vixen stood nearby, watching as Pup's brother tumbled around, scuffing up powdery clouds. Pup and his sister bounded over to her.

"What is all this white stuff, Mummy?" asked Pup.

"It's snow," said Mummy Vixen. "Frozen water that falls from the sky when it's very cold."

Pup placed his paw on the squishy snow and jumped with shock when it sank!

"Can we go and explore?" asked Pup's brother.

"Yes," said Mummy Vixen. "But don't go too far."

"We won't," chorused the cubs.

"And don't leave Pup behind!" she called as they raced off. Pup's brother and sister slowed and waited for him to join them. He was the smallest in the litter and it was a struggle to keep up with the others.

The pups set off into the forest, the sky darkening above them. The crisp, frosty scent filled Pup's nose. To start with it was all he could smell, but soon he began to pick out other familiar scents hiding beneath it. He sniffed out woody pine cones, earthy mushrooms and fresh green shoots, buried below.

"Keep up, Pup!" called his brother.

Pup took a great big leap and caught up with his brother and sister. He trotted along beside them as they carried on through the wintery woods, but soon his legs were aching. He had to take two steps for every one of theirs!

"Mummy said not to go too far," he reminded them.

"I want to get to a high hill so I can see the whole snowy forest," said his brother.

"Don't worry, Pup," his sister reassured him. "We can follow our paw prints all the way home. We won't get lost."

Pup glanced back and sure enough, marks crisscrossed the forest floor.

The cubs walked and walked but no hill appeared. Something chilly tickled Pup's pointy ears. He looked up. Thousands of flakes were floating down from the sky. He watched as his brother's and sister's orange coats became flecked with white, like speckled toadstools. Soon the snow was so heavy that the whole forest seemed to swirl around them.

"Come on," said Pup's sister. "Let's find somewhere to shelter."

They slipped inside a hollow tree, huddling together as the snow fell in flurries outside. Pup peered out at the blizzard, wondering if it would ever stop.

Finally the storm settled, until just a few lazy flakes drifted down. Pup shuffled out of the hollow and caught one on his tongue, going cross-eyed as he tried to examine its special shape.

"We should head home. Mummy will be worried about us." His brother joined Pup outside. "We'll have to go to the hill another time."

"Oh no," said his sister, coming up behind them. "Our paw prints have disappeared! How are we going to find our way back now?"

Pup saw that she was right. The forest floor was smooth once more, with no sign of where their paws had been.

"Come on," said Pup's brother. "I'm sure I'll remember the way."

He set off at a trot. Pup and his sister bounded after their big brother, encouraged by his confident strides. But after several minutes of marching, Pup gazed around at a familiar sight. "Look! There's the hollow tree again," he said.

His sister growled and tackled their brother to the ground. "You've led us round in circles! We're lost!"

Pup peered up at the puffy sky. It looked like the clouds might be about to shake another flurry of snow all over them. What should they do? They couldn't see their way home and they couldn't remember their way home. How were they going to get back? The chilly air filled Pup's nose again. But beneath its frosty scent, Pup noticed another

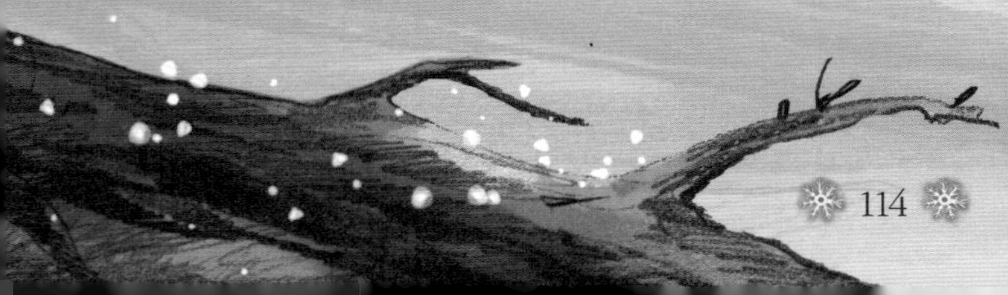

smell… He put his nose to the ground and sniff-snuffled around, searching for something. Aha!

"We need to go this way!" said Pup. "We can't see our paw prints, but I can smell them!"

His brother and sister bounced over, sniffing the ground too.

"Wow, you've got a good nose, Pup!" said his sister.

"Can you get us home?" asked his brother.

"I can try!" said Pup.

The trio set off once again but this time Pup led the way. He pressed his nose so near to the ground that it was soon dusted with the cold, white snow. Still, he didn't give up, following the scent they had left earlier that morning across the forest.

Finally they spotted their ancient hawthorn tree, its roots curling around the entrance to the den. They could see Mummy Vixen's black-tipped ears sticking out as she listened for her little ones' return and they pricked up as the pups approached.

"Where have you been, you silly pups?" she asked, springing towards them.

"We walked too far, then the snow covered our tracks so we couldn't find our way back," said Pup's brother.

"But Pup led us home with his super sniffing!" said his sister.

Mummy Vixen nudged her chilly pups into the den. Beneath the warm earth, the family cuddled up together.

Pup took a big whiff. Of all the interesting scents, the smell of home was his favourite.

"We're fire-furred foxes, whiskered and sharp-eyed,
At night-time we prowl, exploring far and wide.
Our paws leave a trail we can find with a sniff,
To head back home we just follow the whiff."

Owlet and the Song of the Forest

Daddy Owl launched out of the hollow into the sky, just as he did every night when the moon was at its highest point. But this time, Owlet was going to discover where he went! She opened her wings and soared upwards, following Daddy Owl on his flight across the forest. Below her the treetops turned silver in the moonlight. The winding river was a gleaming snake, slithering through the trees.

Daddy Owl swooped down, landing on the topmost bough of the tallest tree. Owlet settled softly beside him, curling her talons round the branch. Daddy Owl turned his head to look at her with his shining black eyes.

"Did you follow me, little one?" he asked. "I didn't even hear a whisper of wings! We're a long way from home."

"I wanted to see where you go every night," said Owlet. "What's so special about this place?"

Daddy Owl blinked. "I come here to listen to the song of the forest."

Owlet had very sensitive ears but she couldn't hear any music.

"What song?" she asked.

"Shhh," said Daddy Owl. "Listen."

Owlet closed her eyes and opened her ears, straining to hear a song. But the sounds of the animals below kept getting in the way!

FLUTTER! Butterfly's wings whir through the air.
HISS! Adder slips and slithers back to his lair.
TOK! Woodpecker bangs his beak on a tree.
BUZZ goes a hard-working honey bee.

SCUFFLE! Rabbit's tired paws burrow below.
FIZZ! Firefly's tail sets the forest aglow.
SNIFF! Fox Cub follows his nose and explores.
GRUNT goes a pair of wallowing boars.

SHRIEK! Bat maps out the wood with his cries.
CHATTER! Squirrel nibbles on a nutty prize.
CROAK! Frog hops off to find a place to roam.
SPLASH goes a beaver kit, fixing his home.

SCRAPE! Mole is on a worm-finding quest.
SQUEAK! Mouse curls up in her hidden nest.
WHIR! Ladybird lets the strong winds steer.
CRUNCH go the footfalls of a little deer.

SWISH! Spider weaves her sparkling threads.
HAAA-WOO! Two wolves throw back their heads.
But what's that last sound, in the cave down there?
Those must be the snores of a sleeping bear!

"Oh!" said Owlet, realizing something. "Those sounds are the song of the forest!"

"That's right," said Daddy Owl. "And what a beautiful song it is."

The two owls huddled up beside each other, their brown speckled feathers blending in among the branches.

"Ke-wick, ke-wick!" called Owlet.

"Hoo-hoo-oo!" replied Daddy Owl. "Hoo-hoo-oo!"

The owls sent their calls out into the night, adding their voices to the song.

Learn more about the amazing creatures we've met in this book...

CATERPILLAR In the first story, Caterpillar turns into a colourful swallowtail butterfly! This particular species has distinctive red-and-blue markings, which look like false eyes to confuse predators!

ADDER Although adders are the only venomous snakes found in the UK, these secretive and timid reptiles rarely bite people.

WOODPECKER Woodpeckers mark their territories by drumming against trees – up to twenty times per second! Their skulls have evolved to make this possible without getting a headache.

RABBIT Rabbit is so happy to return to her side of the river that she does a binky! A binky is when a rabbit jumps up in the air, shakes its head and flicks its paws out.

BLACK BEAR Black bears' strong, curved claws help them climb trees to find food. They also have a long and sticky tongue – perfect for reaching difficult spots like ant colonies!

BEE Bees are nature's gardeners! They spread pollen from plant to plant, helping to make more seeds. Thanks to bees, new flowers, fruits and vegetables can grow.

FIREFLY There are around two thousand species of firefly, each with its own flash pattern. It's an amazing sight!

WILD BOAR Wild boars have big muscles on their chest and the back of their necks that help them dig, and their long snouts help them find food as they root.

BAT Bats find their way around in the dark using echolocation. By making a noise, they can work out the distance and direction of an object from how long it takes for the sound to bounce back.

FROG There are roughly 5,000 species of frog in the world and each one has its own unique call – some of which can be heard up to a mile away. Frogs can also jump up to TWENTY times their own body length!

BEAVER Beavers have very distinct long front teeth, which NEVER stop growing. To stop them from becoming too long, beavers are constantly gnawing.

MOLE Moles have curved front paws and teeth that they use as shovels to dig their extensive underground homes. They can dig up to eighteen feet (five and a half metres) in one hour!

MOUSE For birds of prey, mice are a favourite snack but some species can shed the skin on their tail to escape hungry beaks!

LADYBIRD Ladybirds can eat up to 5,000 aphids and other plant-damaging insects in their lifetime – meaning that farmers love them!

DEER Fawn is so confused as to where his spots have gone. As the average fawn has around three hundred spots that's not surprising! That's a lot of spots to lose.

SPIDER Depending on the species, female spiders can produce egg sacs with up to 2,500 eggs insides! Most spiderlings are eaten before they have a chance to mature – so it's good that Spider can keep an eye on them from her web!

WOLF Wolf packs can only have one alpha male, which is why Black Wolf leaves his pack. When he meets White Wolf, the two of them can start their own pack where they are the alphas.

SQUIRREL Squirrels hide stashes of nuts underground to eat over the winter, but they can lose up to three quarters of these nuts. Sometimes the squirrels forget about them and sometimes they're stolen by other animals – even though squirrels plant decoy stashes to put thieves off!

FOX Foxes can produce twenty-eight different noises to communicate. They also use facial expressions and scent marking!

OWL Owls are practically silent when they fly, thanks to the broad and rounded shape of their wings, allowing them to glide for longer. They also have specially adapted feathers, which reduce the noise of air flowing over their wings.